# Town Mouse and Country Mouse

Written by Gill Budgell

Illustrated by Denise Hughes

# mat

# tap

# off

# hum

# sun

# Talk about the story

Ask your child these questions:

**1** What did Country Mouse find on the mat?

**2** What sound did Town Mouse hear in the country at night?

**3** Why could Country Mouse not get to sleep?

**4** How are Town Mouse and Country Mouse different?

**5** What it the best thing about living in the country? What about the town?

**6** Would you like to live in the country or the town? Why?

Can your child retell the story using their own words?